MINI COLOR SERIES

Russia's T-80U
Main Battle Tank

Text by Steven J. Zaloga & David Markov
Photos & Scale Drawings by Steven J. Zaloga
Color profiles by Hubert Cance

Copyright © 2000
by CONCORD PUBLICATIONS CO.
603-609 Castle Peak Road
Kong Nam Industrial Building
10/F, B1, Tsuen Wan
New Territories, Hong Kong
www.concord-publications.com

We welcome authors who can help
expand our range of books. If you
would like to submit material,
please feel free to contact us.

We are always on the look-out for new,
unpublished photos for this series.
If you have photos or slides or
information you feel may be useful to
future volumes, please send them to us
for possible future publication.
Full photo credits will be given upon
publication.

ISBN 962-361-656-2
printed in Hong Kong

The T-80U family of battle tanks are currently the most modern and sophisticated in Russia's arsenal. They are the descendents of the older T-80 standard tank which first entered Russian service in 1976. The ultimate version of the T-80B family, the T-80BV, entered service in 1985. The primary focus of this book is on the second generation of T-80 tanks, the T-80U series. The "U" in T-80U stands for *uluchsheniye*, or improved. For readers interested in the earlier series, we would refer them to the Concord book (T-64 and T-80, No. 1031)

The T-80U was developed in the early 1980s under the codename Obiekt 219AS with SKB-2 at the Kirov plant in Leningrad taking care of the hull and the Kharkov design bureau developing the turret and armament. The main improvement offered by this design was the incorporation of a new generation of reactive armor called Kontakt-5. In addition, it used the new Refleks guided tank projectile instead of the Kobra used in the T-80B family, and substituted the 1A45 fire control system for the older 1A33. The T-80U was first accepted for service in 1985 and entered series production in 1987 at the Kirov Plant in Leningrad and the Omsk Tank Plant in Siberia. In parallel to the turbine-powered Obiekt 219S, the Kharkov plant developed a diesel-powered version under the codename Obiekt 478B. About 500 of these were built as the T-80UD from 1987 to December 1991. But 300 of these were still at the factory when the Soviet Union broke up in December 1991, so the T-80UD was a rare type in Soviet service.

The separation of Russia, Ukraine and the other former Soviet republics in 1991 severely disrupted tank production. The Kirov plant in Leningrad (now St. Petersburg) which had been the center of T-80 development and production closed its tank lines, and Russian efforts on the T-80 shifted to the Omsk tank plant in Siberia. The development of the diesel powered T-80s at Kharkov in Ukraine continued. But due to rivalry between Russia and Ukraine in the international arms market, Russia refused to supply tank components to Ukraine, so the Ukrainian tank plant had to develop its own sources of sub-components. As a result, by the mid-1990s, there were two parallel development efforts, the T-80U family in Omsk, Russia, and the T-84 program in Kharkov, Ukraine.

The poor performance of the older T-80BV during the war in Chechnya in 1994-95 unfairly cast the T-80U into disrepute. As a result, in 1995 when the Russian Army decided to standardize on either the T-80U or T-90, the army selected the T-90. They later came to regret this decision, as the T-80U was in many respects a more sophisticated tank with greater development potential than the T-90. The Omsk tank plant was forced to turn most of its attention to winning export orders for the T-80U

since there were few orders from the Russian Army. In many of these foreign competitions, the Omsk designers were competing against its former colleagues from the Kharkov Malyshev tank plant and with the Nizhni Tagil tank plant which manufactures the T-72 and T-90. Omsk has managed to sell T-80 tanks to Cyprus, South Korea, and China, while Ukraine has enjoyed a major order of 320 tanks to Pakistan. In recent years, the Russian Army has reconsidered its decision on the T-80 vs. T-90, and has begun a program under the codename Black Eagle to study a more advanced design based on the T-80U.

The inability of the Russian Army to fund the purchase of tanks through most of the 1990s has forced Russian tank firms to turn their attention to the export market. The large assortment of T-80U variants is a testament to this revolutionary change. The many versions of the T-80U here are all based around a common design. However, there is a considerable variety of options being offered with the T-80U. Much as when purchasing an automobile, it is now possible to buy a T-80U with various features including different engines, different reactive armor or active defense packages, and different fire control systems.

T-80BV

This was the definitive version of the first generation T-80s, and was codenamed Obiekt 219RV. It consisted of the basic T-80B retrofitted with the new Kontakt explosive reactive armor (ERA) developed by NII Stali.

T-80U

The Kontakt ERA on the T-80BV was added on after the design was complete and so was not ideally configured. As a result, a new type of built-in reactive armor was developed by NII Stali in the early 1980s along with a new generation of laminate armor called Kontakt 5. These features were incorporated into the Obiekt 219AS design which was accepted for series production in 1985 as the T-80U. This tank also had many other improvements including the new Brod-M deep wading system. In the early 1990s, a slightly improved version was offered for sale called the T-80U(M). This introduced the Buran-P gunner's thermal imaging sight, and a fire control improvement to permit the use of the newer 9M119M Refleks-M guided tank projectile. In 1999, another improvement package was offered for the T-80U(M) which included the 2A46M-4 version of the 125mm gun, the 1G46M gunner's sight, TO-1KO-4 Buran-R gunner's thermal sight, and other improvements.

T-80UK

This began as a simple command tank version of the T-80U at the KBTM design bureau at the Omsk plant in the late 1980s, carrying both a R-163-50U and R-163-50K radio. In the wake of the troubles in the Russian tank industry, Omsk used this modest program to begin a deeper modernization of the T-80U including the addition of the Shtora electronic defense system, an option for the Agava thermal sight, the AB-1-P28 auxiliary power unit, the TNA-4 navigation system, 1A42 fire control system, the uprated GTD-1250 engine and other upgrades. This became the prime Russian export tank in the mid-1990s.

T-80UE

Many of the features of the T-80UK were expensive and not necessary in tanks not used in the command role. As a result, in 1999, the Omsk plant unveiled the T-80UE which dispensed with some of the T-80UK features such as the command radios, while retaining some of the upgrades such as the Shtora system.

T-80UM-1 Bars (Snow Leopard)

In the late 1970s, the Kharkov design bureau developed the Obiekt 478M prototype fitted with the experimental *Shater* active defense system. Shater did not prove successful, and the KBM design bureau in Kolomna developed the more advanced Arena system in its place. It was first tested on a T-80 in the early 1980s, and first deployed in an experimental series batch on the new T-80UM-1 Bars in 1997. The Snow Leopard resembles the normal T-80U except for the addition of the Arena system.

T-80UM-2

A second active tank defense system was developed by the rival KBP design bureau in Tula in the 1980s called Drozd (Thrush) or *Kompleks 1030M-01* and first deployed on T-55AD tanks of the Soviet Naval Infantry in 1988. In 1997, it was offered as one of the possible options on the T-80U, called T-80UM-2. In 1999, KBP began offering a modernized version called Drozd-2 which uses a new, smaller munition and improved sensors. A new version of the T-80U with this feature was being developed by Omsk at the time this book was written.

T-84 Supertank

When the Obiekt 478B was ready for production in 1987 at Kharkov, it was originally planned to call it the T-84. Instead, for simplicity's sake it was called T-80UD. After Ukraine split from Russia in 1991, Russia would not provide cast turrets to the Kharkov tank plant. So the Kharkov plant fell back on a welded turret design planned for the Obiekt 478D, as well as the more powerful 1,200 hp 6TD-2 diesel engine. This improved T-80UD was codenamed Obiekt 478K and later designated as T-84 to distinguish it from the Russian T-80U family. To further confuse matters, the tanks sold to Pakistan were codenamed as Obiekt 478E, but retained the T-80UD name. The first batch used the original cast turret, but later batches used the welded turret of the T-84. Although it resembles the T-84, these tanks are without the Shtora, the uprated 6TD-2 engine and other expensive features

that the Pakistani Army could not afford.

T-84U

The T-84U is yet another improvement to the Obiekt 478 family, but with a new, uprated engine, and many small improvements in the armor package, fire controls and other onboard systems. It was first demonstrated in 1999. Instead of the KBA-3 gun fitted to the T-84, the Ukrainians are offering several armament options including the improved Type 50L Vityaz 125mm gun and the Type 55L Bagira 140mm gun.

Black Eagle

Chorniy Oryol or Black Eagle is the project name for an improved T-80U derivative developed by the KBTM design bureau in Omsk in the late 1990s. This uses a new generation of built-in reactive armor called Kaktus and a new turret design. In contrast to earlier members of the T-80U family, the Black Eagle autoloader is fitted into a turret bustle, not in the hull. A mock-up was first shown in 1997 and an unfinished prototype was displayed in Siberia in June 1999. At the time this book was written, the definitive version had not emerged, and there is still debate on some of its systems including whether to use the Arena or Drozd 2 active defense system, and whether to use a 125mm or 152mm gun. In recent years, Omsk and Nizhni Tagil have begun to cooperate in tank development so some of the Black Eagle features may appear on the T-90 follow-on. In addition, Omsk has offered to mount the Black Eagle turret on a normal T-80U hull rather than on the extended Black Eagle hull.

2S19 Msta-S

The 2S19 Msta-S is a self-propelled 152mm gun based on a modified T-80 hull with the 2A64 gun in an automated turret. Although using T-80 running gear, it is powered by the diesel engine used in the T-72 family. The 2S19 went into production before the collapse of the Soviet Union, and is now being offered with a modified gun tube capable of firing 155mm standard NATO ammunition.

BREM-80U

BREM-80U is a new armored recovery vehicle based on the T-80U hull. It was first displayed in 1997 and is reminiscent of heavy ARV designs in the West such as the BergeLeopard or LeClerc ARV rather than the lighter types with simple jib cranes often deployed in Russia in the past. The vehicle is fitted with a large crane on the front left corner with 18 tons capacity. The superstructure at the front of the vehicle contains a heavy winch for extracting vehicles in conjunction with a bow mounted bulldozer blade. The winch has 35 tons pulling capacity and a 1 ton capacity auxiliary winch for lighter tasks. The vehicle is fitted with a work platform over the engine deck with welding equipment and spare part stowage. The Kharkov tank plant has developed a prototype of its own ARV, based on the T-80UD/T-84.

The most common version of the T-80 family in service at the time of the Soviet Union's collapse was the T-80BV. This version was fitted with Kontakt explosive reactive armor (ERA). This is a view of a tank from the Group of Soviet Forces-Germany (GSFG) being withdrawn to Russia in April 1992. It is an interesting view as the normal skirts are removed exposing details of the running gear. (Michael Jerchel)

The last of the GSFG tanks were withdrawn from Germany in 1994. This is a T-80BV on a railroad flat-car in the Berlin-Lichtenberg station. The vehicles in this September 1994 rail convoy were more colorfully painted than normal service vehicles in a three color scheme of gray, brown and green, and had Russian flags prominently painted on the turret sides for the withdrawal ceremony. The T-80BV was armed with the 2A46M-1 125mm gun with the 1A33 fire control system. (Michael Jerchel)

A close-up of the engine deck of the T-80BV shows details of the reactive armor array as well as the mounting frames for spare fuel drums on the engine deck. The T-80B had poor mileage due to its heavy fuel consumption, and frequently carried extra fuel drums while on operations. The T-80BV was powered by the GTD-1000TF gas turbine engine which had a maximum output of 1,100 horsepower. (Michael Jerchel)

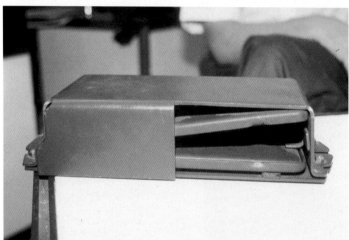

The Kontakt explosive reactive armor consists of hollow metal boxes with two steel plates, lined with plastic explosive. When hit by the jet from an exploding shaped charge warhead, the plastic explosive detonates, throwing the top plate into the warhead stream, and bouncing the bottom plate off the tank's armor to rebound back into the warhead stream. This considerably diminishes the effectiveness of shaped charge warheads on anti-tank rockets or missiles. To prevent peacetime injuries, the explosive panels are not loaded into the boxes until a unit is mobilized for combat action.

In the wake of Chechen attempts to break away from Russia, on the morning of New Year's Eve, 31 December 1994, the Russian Army launched a poorly planned attack on the Chechen capitol of Grozniy. The Russian troops were poorly trained, and in the close confines of the city streets, their tanks were decimated by RPG-7 rockets. This T-80BV in Grozniy has been completely gutted by an internal ammunition fire.

Another view of the same T-80BV burned out in the streets of Grozniy in December 1994. Many of these tanks were knocked out by RPG-7 hits on the rear or engine decks. The Chechen fighters were veterans of the Soviet Army, and knew where the weak points of the tank were located.

Another view of the destroyed T-80BV in Grozniy. This tank suffered an internal explosion from its main gun ammunition which blew the turret off the ring.

Another shot of the same destroyed T-80BV, this time from the front. At least two RPG penetrations are evident on the rear of the turret, which lacked Kontakt protection.

Another T-80BV knocked out in Grozniy during the fighting in Chechnya. In this case, the main gun ammunition suffered a high order detonation which blew the turret in the air, then falling down on the hull on its roof.

Another view of this tank. The subsequent fire has consumed the rubber from the road-wheels.

The same T-80BV near a city tram-car which also suffered from a catastrophic internal ammunition explosion. A penetration is evident on the hull side immediately below the turret.

In the case of this T-80BV, a Russian ordnance team has subsequently inspected the wreck to determine the cause of its destruction, and a white arrow on the side skirt points to one of the penetration points.

A close-up of the turret interior of the T-80BV tank destroyed by a catastrophic ammunition fire, with the massive gun breech of the 2A46M-1 gun evident. Many of the internal fittings have been damaged or burned away.

The reactive armor on the T-80B family was added after the design was complete. In the late 1980s, the T-80U was developed which used the improved Kontakt 5 ERA as well as other internal armor improvements. The international debut of the T-80U was at the IDEX trade exhibition in the United Arab Emirates (UAE) in May 1993. One of the most obvious differences of the T-80U family is the use of the new Kontakt-5 reactive armor. (Christopher Foss)

A T-80U claws its way out of a water obstacle during a demonstration in Siberia in June 1999. Russian tanks are fitted with deep wading gear to permit them to quickly circumvent water obstacles such as streams and rivers.

A T-80U emerges out of a water obstacle during a 1997 demonstration in Siberia at the base of the 242nd Airborne training school near Omsk. This version is still fitted with the Luna L-4A infra-red searchlight, since it lacks a thermal imaging sight.

Water pours off a T-80U as it emerges from a water obstacle. During peacetime exercises, the many stowage items on the turret are often left off, notably the spare ammunition boxes in this case. Evident on the extreme left of the turret is the NSVT machine gun mounting.

A T-80U moments after emerging from a water obstacle. This vehicle is fairly lean and lacks the gun tube thermal sleeve and much of its turret stowage.

In contrast to the T-80U in above photo, this tank has more of its standard stowage fitted including the tank gun thermal sleeve and several of its stowage boxes.

Flying tank! The T-80U has the highest power-to-weight ratio of any current tank, and this is often demonstrated at exhibitions by having the tank jump off an embankment. Seconds later, this tank fired its main gun while in flight, an awesome display even if not very accurate!

This slightly overhead view of a T-80U coming off a hill shows the layout of the Kontakt-5 reactive armor bricks on the roof.

A T-80U moves down along a safety line prior to a firing demonstration at the 242nd Airborne training base in 1999. In this case, the tank has its 12.7mm NSVT heavy machine gun fitted to the pintle mount. Unlike the T-80B which had the NSVT on a remote-control mount, the T-80U uses a simpler pintle mounting which has been found to be more versatile.

A T-80U surmounts a one meter concrete wall while obscured by a smoke grenade from its Tucha smoke mortars.

A T-80U on a gunnery range near Omsk in 1997. The Kontakt-5 armor package extends to the skirts on the front sides of the tank skirts.

An interesting view of a T-80U on a mobility demonstration near Omsk in September 1997. Notice that the Brod-M wading trunk is fastened to the rear of the turret. It can be rapidly fastened over the engine air intakes using an accordion system to speed the time need to prepare to ford a river.

A T-80U in the Siberian Military District in 1999. Russian Army units do not always paint tactical numbers on their vehicles during peacetime, particularly those reserved for public demonstrations. The Omsk bases are near the main plant, and so are the frequent scene of demonstrations for foreign delegations or potential buyers of Russian military equipment.

An ample demonstration of the T-80U's mobility on a test course shows it crossing a one meter obstruction. In Russian service, the T-80U is fitted with metal track, but export clients have been offered a new family of track with rubber or synthetic pads which do less damage on asphalt roads.

A T-80U chews up a water-logged mobility course at the 242nd Airborne training base near Omsk in June 1999.

A T-80U zooms over a hill on a test course during a June 1999 exhibition in Siberia. This gives a good view of some of the roof details.

This particular T-80U is being driven by a test crew from the neighboring Omsk tank plant. The test crews are very skilled tank drivers and put the tank through a rougher pace than would be attempted by young conscript soldiers.

The lower suspension of this T-80U is hidden in the dark soil of the test track. Omsk, along the southern Siberian frontier with Kazakstan, is not affected by permafrost and so has good agricultural conditions.

The T-80U family is fitted with the external AB-1-P28 auxiliary power unit (APU) on he left rear fender which provides 1 kilowatt of electrical power. This unit is under armor and is also called the GTA-18. This is used to operate the tank's electrical systems when the main engine is turned off. The racks to the right of it are mounting racks for fuel drums, and the turbine engine exhaust port.

The low fuel economy of tank turbine engines means that spare fuel is carried on external drums on the hull rear when on operations. This is seldom seen in day-to-day training, and so this picture provides some useful detail on how the drums are connected to the internal fuel system.

While most current NATO tanks are fitted with thermal imaging FLIR night sights, Russia has been slow in adopting this expensive technology. So it was a surprise when the T-80U(M) was first displayed in Nizhni-Novgorod in September 1994 with the Buran thermal imaging sight. This is made somewhat more evident by the fact that the tank is no longer fitted with the normal Luna L-4A infra-red searchlight, and the Kontakt-5 ERA has been extended over towards the gun with an additional small panel.

In recent years, Russia has been moving away from the older MAZ-537 and MAZ-543 family of heavy trucks since they are produced in Belarus. Instead, the Rusich firm has been offering its heavy trucks as a replacement like this massive KZKT-74287 heavy equipment transporter with KZKT-9102 semi-trailer.

One of the features that distinguish the T-80UK is the TShU-1-17 optical jammer, mounted on both sides of the main gun. This is a infra-red emitter that defends against wire-guided anti-tank missiles by confusing the missile launcher's tracker through the use of an intense modulated beam that mimics the tracking flare on the missile. This jammer is part of the Shtora defense system which also includes a laser warning system that triggers smoke grenades.

Starting in 1995, the Russian arms export agency Rosvooruzhenie has been marketing the T-80UK version of the T-80U family. Although nominally a command tank version, it has been placed on offer in the Mid East market for general use since it is fitted with a more extensive array of features than the basic T-80U. This T-80UK is on display in Abu Dhabi in May 1995.

The T-80UK is fitted with a number of other defensive aids as part of the Shora suite including three laser detectors mounted at the 12 o'clock, 4 o'clock and 8 o'clock positions. The Type 902 Tucha smoke mortars have been angled downwards to permit the grenades to bloom faster at a lower altitude. They fire an improved smoke grenade capable of shielding against infra-red sensors.

A T-80UK during its debut at the IDEX-95 exhibition in the United Arab Emirates, The crew is wearing the new pattern brown canvas tanker's helmets which have a different configuration on the sides for new communication head-sets.

A T-80UK on display in Siberia in September 1997 is the same vehicle demonstrated earlier in the UAE. This tank is intended primarily for the export market and has already been sold to China, Cyprus and South Korea.

An overhead view of a T-80UK on display in Abu Dhabi in 1995. The T-80UK is essentially similar to the T-80U, except for the many improvements in the turret.

A T-80UK's sand camouflage paint is not the most appropriate choice for the dark soil of Siberia.

1/35 T-80U MAIN BATTLE TANK

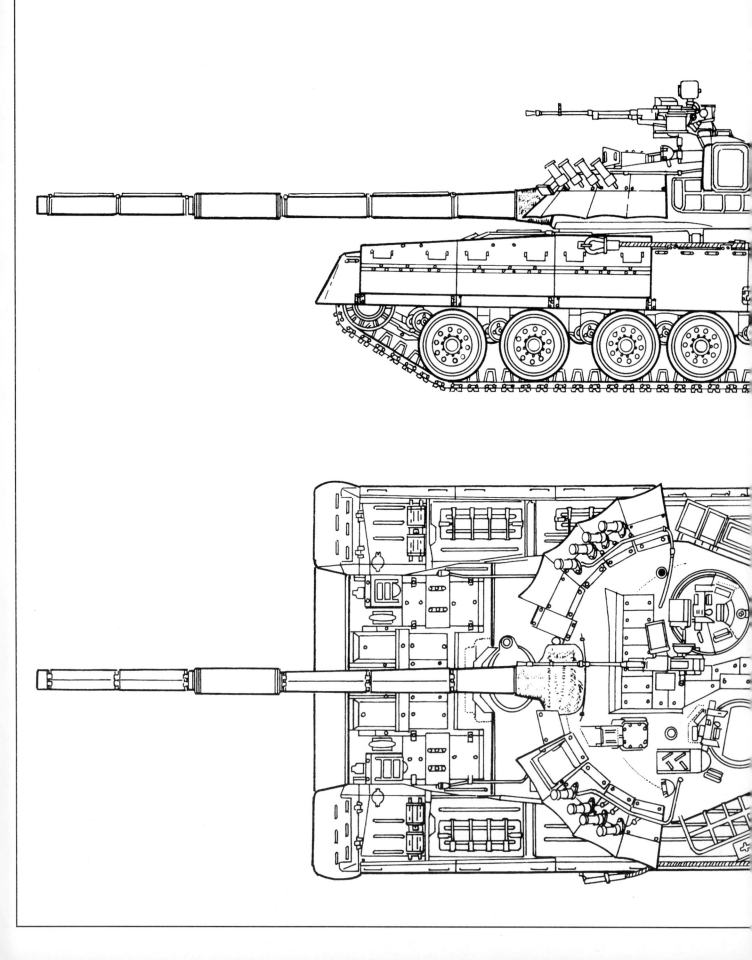

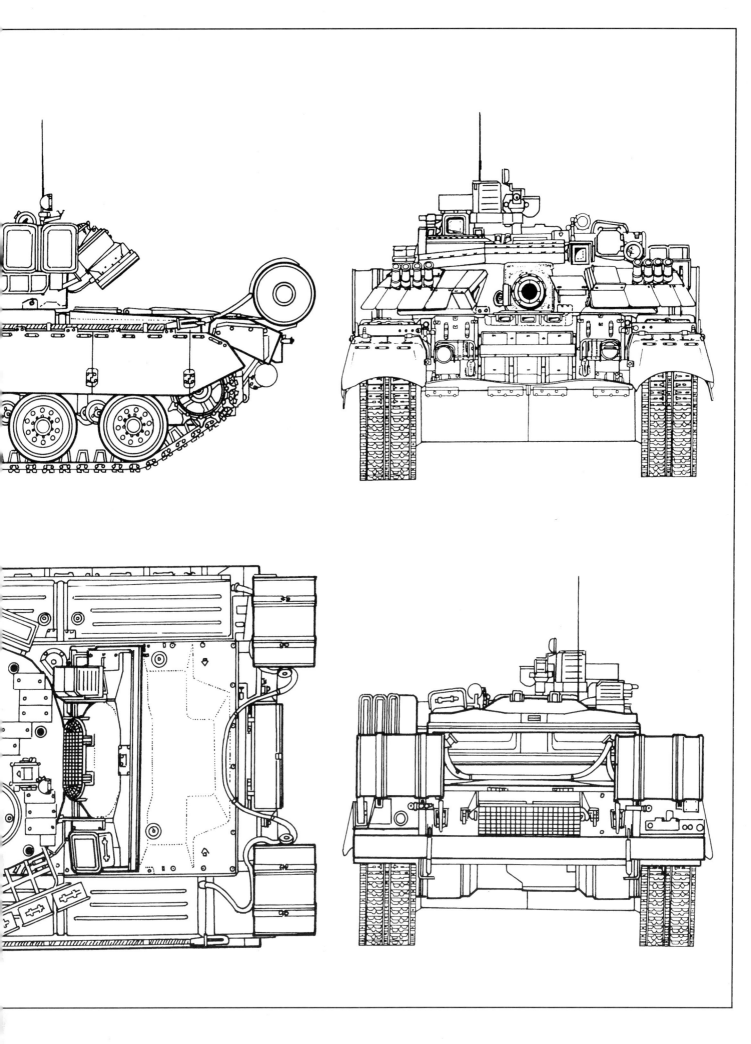

This rear view of a T-80UK near Omsk in September 1997 shows the typical features of the T-80U family including the APU, and turbine exhaust.

A T-80UK moves up to the firing position at the Maqatra range. In the background are the burning wrecks of armored vehicles hit by previous tanks. During this particular exhibition, most of the targets were Iraqi vehicles captured during the Gulf War and sold by Kuwait as scrap.

The T-80UK begins a firepower demonstration on the UAE Army's Maqatra firing range in May 1995. In the background is a 35mm Oerlikon cannon which was also used during the demonstration. The IDEX show is the premier ground forces show in the Mid East and is intended for army officials from many countries interesting in purchasing new equipment.

The T-80UK passes the revetments used for small arms exhibits as it moves out to the firing position at Maqatra.

An interesting shot as the T-80UK moves past showing the elaborate Brod-M deep wading trunk on the back of the T-80UK turret.

The T-80UK during its firing demonstration. The tank is partly obscured by the thermal plume from its turbine engine. Careful inspection of the photo will reveal the tracer beacon at the rear of the Refleks guided projectile that the tank has just fired immediately to the lower right of the MT-LB target. Less than a second later, the MT-LB was destroyed.

A rear view of the T-80UK after its firing demonstration at Maqatra. To the right is a UAE Army BMP-3 with its demonstration crew in blue coveralls. The T-80UK crew is wearing normal Russian Army camouflage uniforms.

The T-80UK on the mobility demonstration course in Abu Dhabi in 1997 still airborne after speeding over a small rise. The Russian tanks are a popular feature at the IDEX shows as they are driven in an aggressive and spectacular fashion with many exciting leaps and bone-crunching landings.

A T-80UK during an exhibition near Omsk in September 1997. In this case, the 12.7mm NSVT heavy machine gun is fitted on the right front pintle. On the T-80UK there are several pintle locations for the machine gun, but it is normal fitted as seen here.

A T-80UK during the 1997 VTTV demonstration near Omsk prior to its firing run. This sand-gray paint finish is strictly for export, and is not a normal scheme on Russian tanks.

A T-80UK moves through the muddy soil on the mobility course at the 242nd Airborne training base near Omsk in September 1997. The speed of the vehicle can be gauged by the angle of the radio antennas and flag.

A view inside the gunner's station of a T-80UK. The sight block to the left with the small video monitor is part of the Agava thermal imaging sight and to the right is the 1G46 Irtysh day-sight/Refleks guidance unit which also incorporates a laser rangefinder. The interior of Russian tanks are very cramped by western standards, though the T-80UK is more spacious than the T-72 and T-90 family.

A view looking from the commander's station in the T-80UK towards the gunner's station in the left hand side of the turret. The top rear corner of the gun breech, painted yellow is barely evident in the lower right corner, with the safety plate in white behind it. The turret rear contains electrical equipment for the autoloader, ammunition data devices and other fire control sub-components.

A view inside the commander's station in the T-80UK shows the commander's PNK-4S Agat day/night sight in the center, with the cupola periscopes on either side. In the T-80UK, the commander can operate the main gun if necessary. Barely visible under the sighting complex is a small monitor from the optical adjunct of the Agava thermal imaging sight which allows the commander to use the gunner's Agava sight at night for observation.

A view from the gunner's station over towards the commander's station on the right side. The cavities in the turret padding are for ammunition, and additional ammunition tubes can be seen in the upper right, along with a green 12.7mm machine gun ammunition box.

During the June 1999 VTTV exhibition at Omsk, one of the T-80UK had been refinished in more conventional Russian Army colors of sand-gray, olive drab and black. The intense thermal bloom of the turbine engine is evident in this view, obscuring the view behind the tank.

The T-80UK comes down off a small hill, providing a look at its upper details.

Another interesting overhead view showing the roof details of the T-80UK including the roof-mounted reactive armor.

In 1999, the Omsk design bureau unveiled the T-80UE for the first time. This has many of the features of the T-80UK command tank, but lacks the redundant command radios and many of its more expensive upgrades. One of its more distinctive features was its garish camouflage finish of bright yellow and a dark purple-brown.

This side view of a T-80UE shows the features it shares with the T-80UK including the Shtora self-protection system.

The T-80UE emerges from a water obstacle at the 242nd Airborne training base near Omsk during the June 1999 demonstration.

T-80BV, Russian Army, GSFG, Berlin, Germany, 1992

During the pull-out of the Russian Army from Germany in 1992, a number of departing units painted their vehicles in more elaborate camouflage and markings than was normally the practice. In this case, this tank regiment added bands of gray and red-brown over the usual dark olive green (*zeleno-zashchitniy*) camouflage color. They also marked the tanks in the new Russian tri-color flag to distinguish themselves from the former Soviet Army.

T-80U(M), Russian Army, Nizhni-Novgorod, 1993

In the mid-1980s, the Soviet Army adopted a new three color camouflage scheme similar in appearance to the US Army's 1970 MERDC scheme. The new pattern used a special paint developed by NII Stali which reduced the probability of detection to electro-optical sensors operating in the near infra-red bands. The three colors in this pattern are dark olive green (*zeleno-zashchitniy*), yellow-gray (*sero-zheltiy*), and black (*cherniy*).

T-80UE, Russian Army, Siberian Military District, 1999

Some new tanks manufactured in Omsk in 1997-1999 have been painted in this colorful scheme of dark purple-brown with bright yellow bands. The reason for the scheme is not at all clear, and may simply be intended to stand out at vehicle demonstrations.

T-84U, Ukrainian Army, Abu Dhabi, 1999

The T-84 has appeared in a special desert demonstration scheme when displayed in the Mid East, this consists of a bright mustard yellow with swatches of field drab and black.

King of the hill ! The T-80UE races over a hill on the mobility track near Omsk.

As the T-80UE moves down the hill, it reveals some of the details of its roof area. The roof configuration is much the same as on the T-80UK. However, there are differences, such as the use of the older type of cross-wind sensor at the rear of the turret.

The T-80UE is moved to its staging area in a demonstration of the new Russian KZKT-74287 heavy equipment transporter with KZKT-9102 semi-trailer.

The business end of the T-80UE shows the low, lean lines of this tank. With its Kontakt-5 armor, this tank has protection levels from the front comparable to those of the M1A1 Abrams or Leopard 2.

A good view of the garish paint scheme of the T-80UE. This scheme is probably intended for public demonstration rather than for actual service use.

This view of the T-80UE on a mobility demonstration near Omsk in 1999 gives a view of some of the upper details of the tank including the new gunner's sight. The fire truck is in the background as munitions used during the firepower demonstration such as smoke grenades sometimes set grass fires.

A nice head-on shot of the T-80UE reveals its sleek lines. Careful examination of the area immediately above the gun barrel will reveal the earlier pattern cross-wind sensor instead of the later stalk-mounted type.

Silhouetted against the sky, this view shows the prominent Brod deep wading trunk on the turret rear, as well as the pintle mounted heavy machine gun.

Like the T-80UK, the T-80UE has the Tucha smoke mortar arrays angled downward. The external differences between the T-80UE and T-80UK are subtle.

A line up of vehicles in the Siberian military district from left to right, including a BMP-2, BMP-3, T-80UK and T-80UE.

The T-80UM-1 Bars (Snow Leopard) is the first member of the T-80U family fitted with an active defense system. The belt around the turret is part of the Arena active defense system, as is the sensor mast at the rear of the turret roof.

The T-80UM-1 Snow Leopard was the first of the Omsk T-80U variants to sport this garish yellow and olive drab camouflage scheme. This view provides a good look at the large active radar/passive IR missile warning array on the roof.

The T-80UM-1 Snow Leopard is pulled out of a water obstacle by a BREM-1 recovery vehicle. The BREM-1 is based on the T-72 chassis.

A T-80UM-1 Snow Leopard with a BREM-1 recovery vehicle in the background during its September 1997 debut near Omsk.

A view of the left hand side of the T-80UM-1 Snow Leopard. This vehicle shares many features with the T-80UK except the Arena system to the turret.

A T-80UM-1 Snow Leopard passes by a TMM-6 heavy bridge during its mobility display. The two devices immediately above the gun barrel are laser warning sensors which trigger the smoke grenades if the tank is targeted by a hostile laser designator.

A close-up view of the rear of the T-80UM-1 Snow Leopard turret shows the usual Brod-M wading trunk, the extra 12.7mm ammo boxes on the wading trunk, the Arena sensor, the right side laser sensor, and the side stowage.

This close-up of the front of the T-80UM-1 Snow Leopard shows the Kontakt-5 array on the glacis plate as well as the skirt of explosive cassettes around the turret.

This overhead shot of the turret front of the T-80UM-1 Snow Leopard shows the reactive armor panels on the roof. The device immediately behind the gun tube is a pair of laser warning receivers.

This close-up view shows the explosive cassettes that are loaded into the armored skirt around the turret. When activated by the radar sensors, these fire up into the air one at a time, and are detonated by a trailing wire. They explode like a claymore mine, spraying any anti-tank missiles below them with a destructive blast of metal fragments.

The heart of the Arena system is this millimeter wave radar which detects the approach of incoming anti-tank missile. It passes this data to an onboard computer processor which then selects one of the explosive panels, which is launched to destroy the missile. The vertical sensor behind the Arena radar is a standard cross-wind sensor, while the electro-optical sensor below it is part of the tank's laser warning system.

Another new version of the T-80U family revealed in September 1997 was the T-80UM-2. This is similar to the basic T-80U but is fitted with the Drozd-1 active defense system. The Drozd (Thrush) fires rocket projectiles to intercept incoming anti-tank missiles, and the red plastic covers of those launchers can be seen in this front view.

This side view clearly shows the features of the Drozd-1 system including the launcher array as well as the processor unit for the system mounted in an armored box on the left rear side of the turret.

A T-80UM-2 passes by signs at a mobility track of the 242nd Airborne training center near Omsk in Siberia in 1997. The signs are used to identify obstacles on the course.

This rear view of the T-80UM-2 shows the typical T-80U features, but also provides details of the processor unit used by the rocket launcher array.

A right side view of the T-80UM-2 during a mobility demonstration showing the stowage on the right side of the turret. Notice that the processor unit for the launchers is carried only on the left turret side. On previous tanks fitted with the Drozd system such as the T-55AD, the processor unit was mounted on the rear of the turret. This is not possible on the T-80U since it is fitted with the Brod-M wading trunk.

A comparative view of the T-80UM-2 from the left side showing the turret stowage.

The crew of the T-80UM-2 take a cigarette break. They wear two different patterns of camouflage coveralls, the type on the right being the more common pattern.

A detail view of the T-80UM-2 from the right rear showing the usual stowage rack for the external fuel drums.

A detail view from the rear of the Drozd launcher. The assembly at the top is the millimeter wave radar detector which locates and identifies incoming anti-tank missiles. The two assemblies below are the 107mm KAZ rocket launchers.

This front view shows the four right side rocket launchers and the radar array above. On determining the location and impact time of the incoming anti-tank missile, the Drozd system launches one of the 3UOF14 rockets which then detonates at seven meters in front of the tank, spraying the anti-tank missile with a pattern of metal fragments.

A detail view of the left side Drozd array on the T-80UM-2. In 1999, the new Drozd-2 system was first revealed which uses a more compact rocket launcher system with more tubes, and a more sophisticated radar sensor. It is being incorporated into a follow-on version of the T-80UM-2.

Ukraine's Kharkov tank plant manufactured the diesel powered T-80UD prior to the Soviet collapse in 1991. In recent years, Ukraine has restored the plant by replacing Russian-manufactured components with local components. Its new T-84 uses a locally manufacture welded turret instead of the cast turret found on Russian T-80Us.

Pakistan is the first customer for the T-80UD from Ukraine, buying 320 of these tanks. The first vehicles arrived in March 1997 and were configured with the original cast turret. Later batches were fitted with the angular welded turret used on the T-84. These are known internally as Obiekt 478F, the "F" indicating export.

The crew of a Ukrainian T-84 during a display in Abu Dhabi in May 1995, sitting next to an upgraded T-72AG. This display helped win Ukraine a contract for 320 T-80UD tanks for Pakistan. The Pakistani T-80UDs are similar to the T-84, but lack some of the expensive features such as the Shtora defense system.

A view of the T-84 from the right side. This T-84 prototype had many Russian components, but later production vehicles began to use more Ukrainian parts. Notice that the T-84 retains the remote control 12.7mm NSVT heavy machine gun instead of the simple pintle mounts used on the Russian T-80U tanks.

This overhead view of the turret gives a good indication of the many changes incorporated into the T-84 compared to its Russian cousin, the T-80U. It is fitted with a Ukrainian equivalent of Kontakt-5 reactive armor. The smoke dischargers are under a thin armor cover. The small blue and yellow insignia is the Ukrainian Army marking, the trident of Volodymir.

Aside from the welded turret, the most significant difference between the Ukrainian T-84 and Russian T-80U is the powerplant. The T-84 uses a 6TD diesel engine, a modernized version of the powerplant first developed for Kharkov's T-64 tank.

A rear view of the T-84 accentuates the many small external differences between the Ukrainian and Russian versions of the T-80 family since the Ukrainian tanks use a very different pattern of external stowage bins.

From the front, the T-84 is very similar to the Russian T-80U family, except for the distinctive smoke mortar arrays.

This close-up shows the details of the smoke mortar arrays. The box behind the Kontakt-5 reactive armor is the power supply for the Shtora anti-missile jammer.

This overhead detail view shows the Shtora emitter on the right side of the T-84 turret as well as overhead details of the Kontakt-5 reactive armo.

Due to its use of the 6TD diesel engine, the T-84 uses a fundamentally different engine deck than the turbine powered Russian T-80U tanks. The pattern is much more similar to that on the original T-80UD.

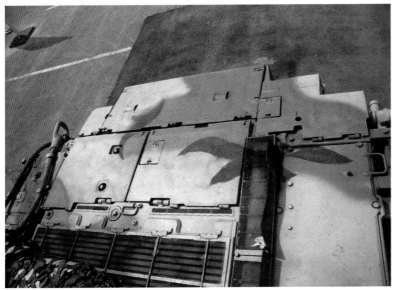

A right front view of the T-84U shows some of the changes including the new side skirts which extend down further than on the T-84 or T-80U.

In May 1999, Ukraine revealed its new T-84U tank at the IDEX exhibition in the UAE. This vehicle is based on the T-84 but uses entirely Ukrainian components. It also incorporates a number of improvements. One of the changes evident on this view is the addition of a new auxiliary power unit, contained in the armored box at the rear of the right fender.

This left front view shows some of the other changes including the slightly different configuration of the Kontakt-5 panels on the turret front and the addition of a small reference radar antenna near the gunner's hatch, used to measure the speed of the tank gun projectile to compensate for barrel wear.

The deeper skirts and Ukrainian pattern stowage give the T-84U a distinctly different appearance from the Russian T-80U tanks.

A T-84U during a mobility demonstration in Abu Dhabi. This view reveals the new rubber padded tracks being offered on the T-84U, a requirement in many countries to minimize road damage.

The T-84U races down a hill during the mobility trials. As can be seen in this view, the Kontakt-5 reactive armor panels are smaller and of a different shape to better conform to the T-84U's welded turret.

The T-84U emerges from a water obstacle at the May 1999 IDEX exhibition. The IDEX show in the UAE has established the international standard for tank exhibitions with an exciting mobility display filled with obstacles, obstructions and other features to better demonstrate the tank's automotive performance. (IDEX)

This side view provides a good idea of the differences between this version and earlier T-80U and T-84 types.

This side view from the right shows how the skirts have been extended downward. The turret stowage on the Ukrainian T-84 family is distinctively different from the Russian T-80U family.

A good head-on shot of the T-84U shows how the Ukrainians have added ERA panels in the space between the gun mantlet and the Shtora missile jammers.

The T-84U uses a somewhat different applique armor than the Kontakt-5 on the Russian T-80U family. The turret panels are smaller, and the glacis plate panel is flush without the distinctive "chocolate bar" levels seen on the T-80U.

A T-84U is fueled up from a UAE Army bowser with a mosque and minaret evident in the background.

In 1997, the Omsk tank plant revealed its Black Eagle tank at the September VTTV exhibition. The tank made a very brief pass in front of the reviewing stands and then disappeared.

The turret of the Black Eagle was covered with camouflage netting and a canvas tube over the gun to hide its details. In fact, this vehicle is only a crude mock-up, as would be revealed later.

As is evident from these views, the original Black Eagle mock-up was based on the hull of a standard T-80U. The only difference was the turret mock-up.

In June 1999, the Black Eagle made another appearance. Here it is seen on its MAZ-537 tank transporter, its turret still hidden under camouflage netting.

The Black Eagle shown in 1999 was fundamentally different from the 1997 vehicle, being based on a new lengthened hull with an extra road-wheel on each side. It also uses the new Kaktus reactive armor on the turret.

The Black Eagle is initially fitted with a standard 125mm gun, though there have been rumors that it will later be fitted with a larger gun, perhaps in 152mm caliber.

One of the most distinctive features of the Black Eagle is the large turret bustle which contains an autoloader for the main gun.

The Black Eagle prototype on display in June 1999. This view clearly shows the elongated hull with seven road wheels.

Illustrations of the Black Eagle have shown it fitted with both an Arena active defense system, and with the new Drozd-2 system. This is a model of the Desert Eagle, a version of the Black Eagle fitted with the Drozd-2 active defense system. The launchers are mid-ways on the turret side.

The first public exhibition of the 2S19 to an international audience was at the Moscow air show in 1992. It is finished in the standard scheme of sand-gray, olive green and black. The device at the rear of the turret is an external autoloader, designed to make it easier to reload the internal auto-loading cassettes.

The 2S19 Msta-S is one of the more distant relations of the T-80U family. It is based on a modified T-80U chassis, but powered by the diesel engine from the T-72 series. Here, its 2A64 152mm gun is shown at full elevation during an exhibition in Nizhni-Novgorod.

The 2S19 Msta-S has been exhibited on many occasions overseas, but has not yet won a major international sale. Here it is being demonstrated on the mobility track at the IDEX show in the UAE.

Another view of the 2S19 Msta-S at Abu Dhabi. As is evident in this view, the 2S19 uses the running gear of the T-80 series, but even the wheel spacing is different to better absorb the different loads of the 2S19 system.

A 2S19 Msta-S moves up to the firing line at the UAE Army's Maqatra firing range. As impressive as it is in indirect fire, the 2S19 is even more impressive attacking armored targets in short-range direct fire with its massive 152mm gun. In the background is a BTR-80A.

Troops from the UAE Army inspect the 2S19 Msta-S after the firing exhibition. The Russians have offered a 155mm version of the 2S19 in the hopes of enticing foreign customers who already use NATO caliber ammunition. A wide range of ammunition is available, including laser-guided Krasnopol projectiles.

A 2S19 Msta-S leads a column, followed by a T-80UK. This view shows some of the features shared with the T-80 including the track and front entrenching blade.

The BREM-80U is the recovery version of the T-80U family. It was first displayed in 1997 but has not yet been widely deployed in the Russian Army. The configuration is more similar to NATO ARVs than earlier Russian designs, with a hydraulic crane on the right, and a large compartment with winch equipment in the center.

This left side shot shows the general configuration of the BREM-80U including the trunk for the fording system on the rear deck.

The crew of the BREM-80U prepare the crane for a lifting operation while assisting in the erection of a TMM-6 bridge during an exercise in Siberia in 1997.

A BREM-80U on display near Omsk in 1997, being followed by a BTR-T heavy infantry vehicle.

A detail view of a BREM-80U on static display at the Polyot plant in Omsk in 1999 during the June VTTV exhibition. This shows the large hydraulic crane located on the right side of the vehicle.

A rear view of the BREM-80U shows the usual turbine exhaust port so characteristic of the T-80U series as well as the familiar Brod-M wading trunk behind the service compartment.

An interesting overhead shot of the front right side of the BREM-80U showing details of the service compartment and crane.

A companion shot of the BREM-80U from overhead on the right side showing details of the crane and rear deck stowage.